T0078395

Spring Flowers

Nadia Nawrin

To order additional copies of this book, contact:
Xlibris
844-714-8691
www.Xlibris.com
Orders@Xlibris.com
550349

Dedications

To My Loving Grandparents.

"My soul was quivering to speak
Thousands of unspoken words
So I gave it a pen and paper
And asked to begin its journey"

Nadia Nawrin

Contents

"Soften your heart
Loosen your mind
As you slowly enter
The journey of blossom"

Nadia Nawrin

Irreversible Moments

Like a slow-moving wave
I have begun to walk on this path
The memories of these irreversible moments
Are seeming to be written like a plage

Without a Shining Knight

Not every story will have a happy ending
Nor it will have a prince charming
There are times in life where
We must make the
Unexpected a part of our lives
And learn to fight without a shining knight

Grieve

Life is filled with
Unexpected feelings
We thirst for our happiness
Through sadness
And grieve the person
When they are gone

Moon Whispering To The Night

I sat by the window quietly
listening to the moon whispering to the night
A beautiful sound of the wave dancing
Through the ocean
And cackling with the wind

I can feel the cool breeze touching my face
And swiping around my hair
I watched the beautiful love
Between the moon and the night
As the ocean danced under the moonlight

Light Of Hope

I can still remember crying
And lost in a tunnel
My heart was
filled with deep prayers
And softly sobbing

That moment felt so oblivion
As if the darkness had
Surrounded me from everywhere

Until I have learned
To build my courage
From these deviance moments
And search for the light of hope

Reverberates

I can hear the reverberates
Of the soft mist down by the bay
My soul began to dance like
A whirlpool of happiness
I let myself wander off
To search for the moment of bliss

Intoning

I remember the soft intoning voice
Of my mother as she embraced
Every hardship to her soul
She would lift her chin
And hid all her sorrow
She would gently
Swirled around my hair
And with her soft red lips
Kissed me good nights

Clamouring

Even if the days were filled
With darkness clouds and
The thunder roaring down
The moment felt so clamouring
As my father held my hand down

Myriad Calls

I was told beyond those
Mystical doors there are
Myriad calls asking me
To chant away the softness
Of innocence prayers
And letting my soul wonder
For the peace that belongs here

Elusive

Through the dusk of the night
An elusive of hope has been
Enchanting my soul
As I closely embraced
The moment close to my heart
I felt the ease of my mourning
Has begun to dissolve

Blue Sapphire

For years I was searching
For relics love and my faulty stars
I've caged my inner self
Away to be alone
And taunted me
As I have been lost

Until I began to find
The blue sapphire inside of me
Filled with alluring light and
Charming glee

In the rhythm of gleaming
Gasping away my joy
As I found myself again
And I am
The blue sapphire

Gladden

A mystical momentum
humming upon my name
My soul has begun to fly
The moments of gladden
has swathed me into its' arm

Poignant

It was not so long ago
I sat by the river
Wondered the poignant moments
I was put through
Then I realized it was
Never me that they were jealous of
It was my inner aptitude
They had envied

Luminous

I have painted a luminous art
Where I have wings to fly
And freedom to scream
My desire of being free is painted
On the canvas on the wall
And when you look deep into the art
You can see the luminous glow of me

Sail

They left me in an empty boat
To sail myself on the ocean of boundlessness
I felt the fear of loneliness
Gasping my chest
They left me alone to drown
Into my own dread

I stood up tall
And fixed my sailor hat
As the wind began to blow
I have sailed the boat
Back to the shore

I knew deep inside
I was never alone
The one I needed
Has been listening
To my prayers all along

Dancing

As the sun began to rise
I can feel the cool breeze
Swirling over the mountain
I slowly began to dance
As the rain
Poured down softly

Garden

There is a secret door
To the garden of harmony
Thus I began to search
For the key

They say the garden
Holds the most precious flowers
That only blossom
In spring

Courage

For years I kept my courage
Locked inside a box
Every day I would peek inside
And quickly hid it away

I was told not to carry it with me
As it was too fragile
For the world to see
But one day my courage
Decided to escape
From all these deceive

It looked me into the eyes
And asked "let's rise together"

Verses

As I opened the chapters
And slowly set out to read
I began to feel
The soothing feeling
Surrounding me

My heart felt the mystical
Vibe of happiness
As I was reluctant not to smile

I embarked to enjoy
Verses of the book
While it enfolded
The power over me

Sweet Companion

I longed for a friend who
I can call my own
I would share the true feelings
And concur the love of all
I was blessed
With someone like you
Whom I call a sister
And a sweet companion
of my own

Calligraphed

There is a canvas of your name
Beautifully calligraphed with black ink
I imagined your soft skin
With dark brown eyes
Twinkling to see
As I slowly closed your eyes
And forever calligraphed
Your name in me

Lanterns

Across the shore
Far away land
I can see thousands of lanterns
Has been set free
Each lantern had the name of me

Petal

As the rose began
To lose its petal
I sat beside it
And watched
The beauty of it
Vanish away

I held it close to me
With teary eyes
And the fragrances of it
Reminded me
A beauty of a rose
Never dies

Hidden

Thousands of words
Were hidden behind that smile
Only if you held her hand
A bit longer you would have known
The struggles of her own

Empty Pages

The empty pages of my heart
Was thriving to write
As I gave it a pen to began
It flourished the pages

With memories of you & I

Blessings

Beyond the blurry edges
A softness of love
Chanting and echoing the
Prayers of your lips had thirsts
It sends away the blessings
Through the whistling of the wind
Before you open your eyes remember
The one

Memory Lane

Going down by the memory lane
My soul has recollected
All the verses that once were hidden
I found the person I had lost back then

Love Letters

As I began to enfold the letters
I can feel the mystical essence
Whistling around the room
I looked upon the words
As it was filled with so much love
The softness of the peaceful moment
Wrapped me into its arm
As I began to enfold the letters
I felt the energy of calm

A Tale of Broken Wings

Her wings were broken
As she fought
like a warrior
To them, she was a threat
Thus with lies they
Hid all the truth beneath the sky
Deep down she knew
Wings can only be tied down
But the soul of a warrior
Can never be broken down

Captain Of The Boat

From the faraway land
A little boy comes and sits
By the shore each day
Listening to the wind
Romping over the sea
With wondering eyes
He would lookup
At the sky and smile
The little boy knew his destiny
Was just by the sea
Yet he would dream to
Sail away from the shore
As he imagined to be
The captain of the boat

The Nectar Of My Love

I held on my hand
The nectar of my love
And let myself lost into the
Devine of transcendent devotion
It rambles me into its arm
As I dive more into the nectar of love

The Child

One day you will look back
To the days you were being silly
The days you played with mud
And ran around playing tags
You will look back to the child
You have left behind
A memory filled with
Joy yet ache of sighs

Engraved

You can see in the eyes of wound
The pain of losing someone so deep
The tears are not so ordinary
It's the memory of whom
Engraved into the heart forever

Emptiness

When I lost you
I've lost the soul in me
The endless pain of emptiness
Forced me into the darkness
Just once I wanted to ask you
Are you fine my dear?

Autumn

It was the month of October
The leaves began to fall
And the roads were
Decorated with different
Shades of colours
It looked so mesmerizing
The beauty of the autumn
Reminded me of you
As I looked myself into the mirror

Keep Smiling

Keep smiling my dear
You're doing great
All the miles
You've walked alone
Let your brave soul
Take you ahead

Rhythm

I let my heart
Dance to the rhythm
Of the music
Under the moonlight
And the shooting stars

Stories

Keep telling your stories
And don't stop
Despite the troublesome
They may have caused

Your inspiring bravery
Will awake thousands of souls
You may be alone today
But one day it will be us all

Stolen

A heart cannot be stolen
Until you gave it away
Love cannot be mistaken
Until you looked away

Darkness Flame

Don't stop the flame
That is burning through the darkness
Let the light of this burning flame
Take you through the path you have walked alone
Don't let your inner self
Stop you from the trauma you have survived
Let the flame set the darkness on fire
And light up every path you may take

Detox

Sometimes don't just
Detox your inner body
But learn to detox
The negative people
From your life too

Throughout These Years

Throughout these years
There's been lots of
Ups and downs
We've lost so many
Of our dearest ones
And tried to overcome
Our own battles

We didn't know where this road
Was going to take us but
Kept holding onto each other

Although today it's been
So many years together
But still feels like
It's day one all over again

A Corner

A place that does not
Want the presence
Of your sweetness love
Let yourself find
A corner that thrives
For your smile

Door Of Honesty

They tried to keep the
Door of honesty
Hidden away from me
But little do they know
The key to the door belongs to me

Masterpiece

A masterpiece of art
Was hung on the wall
It was a story of the painter
Who had fallen in love with his master
It was a forbidden love and he dares to speak of it
Thus he kept the secret hidden inside the colour of his art

Melodies

Sweet humming melodies
Led me to the
Notes of music
Where the piano and the orchestras
Are waiting for me to sing

Invisible Battle

You have fought this
Invisible battle all alone
Thus don't fear what
They may say just to
Break you down once again

Stand on your feet
Guard your defense
Let your intuition
Guide you to the victory stand

Let Her Go

Although the ache of the painIs forever to stayBut the memory ofOur good timesWill never be erasedAs I let her goAnd ease my painI know this love & friendshipWill always be growing

Midnight Story

I sat by the table
Sipping away some hot tea
I let my mind pour down
To the pages

Midnight thoughts have
Its own kind of theme
It's a time of loneliness
Yet it's bittersweet

Your presence of loneliness
Crafts a beautiful story
And that's the beauty
Of a midnight story

Invisible Thorns

It's not the deep wound
That hurts the pain
It's the invisible thorns
I had not seen

NADIA NAWRIN

Field Of Success

As we sift through
The hardship moments of our lives
Our dedication and privation
Will lead us to the field of success

Catastrophe

I have learned to let go of myself
And explore without the fear of catastrophe

Unwind

Unwind your inner soul
As the mystical gust
Wafting around your heart
Let this spiritual call
presume you free

Recalls

Let the memory enjoy the minutes
As it recalls all the
Gifted moments you once had
Captured in a photo frame

Soft Rain

Let the gentle soft rain
Fall upon you
Allow yourself to open the door of unknown abilities
Trying to overcome the power of wisdom
To cast upon your soul
Let the rain dissolve into your skin
As you slowly close your eyes
And smell the soft summer breeze

Over The Mountain

I want to fly over the mountain
And touch the beautiful clouds resting above
I want to feel the soft wind blowing
Onto my face as I slowly inhale and exhale
I want to fly over the mountain
Under the ocean of blue sky
Allow myself to be hypnotize
By the beauty of nature

Own Kind

The sweetness of your heart
Allowed me to be mesmerized
Your softness of words
Has given this friendship
Of its own kind

Revisited

I have revisited the memories
Once upon we lived by
I walked across the river
Where you used to chase me down
I passed by the old bakery
Where you used to love taking me out
I revisited the memories to say one final goodbye
Perhaps it is time I let the memories rest along by your side

Closing The Chapters

As I closed the chapters
Of you and I today
I folded the pages
Where we might want to
Revisit one day
Maybe only this time
We will be reading
The chapters together

Silence

Let the silence
Perform its art of success

Dissolve

Let your sorrow dissolve away
As you have begun to heal
The emptiness you have inside
Will be filled one day
Let your heart begin to cleanse away
And start a new beginning of another day

Like A Bird

Like a bird
I want to be free
And fly where the sun rise

Set my wings free
So I can fly
Across the across the ocean
Over the golden field

Let my wings fly
Where the river flows
Under the beautiful blue sky

Loving Heart

I sat by the swings today
Remembering the old times
Felt like it was just the other days
Chasing and playing on the grass
Memories of those sweet childhoods
Were running through my mind
So many years of this beautiful friendship
Saved on a stone of memory of a loving heart

Melody Of The Flute

I slowly closed my eyes
As I began to listen to the
The musical melody of the flute
There was a deep pain hidden
Somewhere in the tune

I'm Sorry

I'm sorry for the times
I judged you because of others
I'm sorry I did not give you any time
Because I was busy comforting others
I'm sorry I treated you poorly
While I poured my love for others
This time as I am looking into the mirror
I promise myself I will treat myself better

Old Tune

Playing the old tune
On the piano
As I recall the notes
You had written to me
Once, long ago

Wrong Pages

Maybe I was wrong
Or maybe we were both
On the wrong pages

Maybe we just got
Off the bed on the wrong side
Or maybe we both forgot
How to laugh

Maybe we forgot to remind
Each other the love we have
And unwind the misunderstandings
We may have mingled ourselves

Eternity

A beautiful divine moment
Of love hast me into his arms
Thou shall be by my side
For the eternity of this universe

Harness

Sat by the window
At midnight passed two p.m.
Looking up at the beautiful full moon
With sparkling stars
My soul began to harness
With the magnificent moment of
Peace and harmony

Rejuvenate

Let your mindset
In the peaceful silent space
Allow the emotions
To speak on their own
And focus on the
Nurture of your heart
As you feel well centered
And aligned with yourself
Let the mindset
And rejuvenate itself

Relinquish

Relinquish what has been
Hurting your soul
Create a new pathway
To embrace yourself
Let the energy of new love
Bestow upon you
Feel the moment of
The passion that is waiting for you

Beliefs

Let your beliefs walk you
Through the path
Where you hold the
Pen of faith

New Moon

A new moon
Is a new beginning
Thus forget last night
And start a new chapter
Tonight

Shooting Stars

Close your eyes
And wish upon
The shooting stars
Let the miracle
Roll its dice

Captivated

I have captivated these
Unspoken words in me
For over a decade
And now as I watch
Them spread in joy
I want to enthrall this
Moment of my accomplishment
I had thrived

A Picture Of Me

Again I sketched a picture of me
But this time I had a smile

Poisonous Words

Don't let these poisonous words
Enter your ears and disbelieve the believers
And let the truth buried under

Repair

Things may not heal
Right now
But allow your soul
To repair and set free

Workshop

Counting blessings
Are like a workshop
Of good deeds

Paws

The little paws of yours
Has bestowed over me with so much love
A priceless affection of your innocent eyes
Has captured me into this eternity of love

Intricated

As I was lost
beneath the ocean
They intricated the
Stories of me
And
As I was drowning
And losing my breath
A mystical hand
Reached out for help
I slowly opened my eyes
And found myself
By the shore

Impeccable Journey

As the final destination has arrived
The impeccable journey must end
Perhaps this is not a goodbye
But just a new beginning to start

Sacred

Perhaps connecting so deeply
Into this divine of love
Has allowed me to
Recreate my presence

This sacred friendship
Of eternal nurture has
Fond me into this beautiful
Circle of closeness and joy

Coming To An End

As it's slowly coming to an end
Of my journey in
Fate of writing
A humbleness of relieve
Has left from my chest
Perhaps these words
Needed a book to be saved
As I set this journey
Free to fly
I will begin my next journey
In search of my origins
in the fate of writing
I shall find

Spring Flowers

The joy of this manifesting reminiscence
Has showered me into the wonders of love
So many beautiful colours and shades
In the garden of spring flowers

Spring Flowers

Nadia Nawrin

Acknowledgements

Across the horizon, over the ocean, the eternity of tenderness care has always blessed upon me. I thank the Almighty for accepting my prayers. This journey was never possible without my beautiful family and friends. A heartfelt thank you to my publisher; and my lovely readers for reading my poetry and able to rejoice and connect with my thoughts.

About The Book

Spring Flowers is a journey navigating through happiness, sorrow, love, healing, family, friendship, self-growth, and self-love. It's a collection of inspirational poetry bundled in a book. The book was written to express the unspoken words and bloom into the readers' heart.

Printed in the United States
By Bookmasters